BE STILL MY HEART

SHAKU SELVAKUMAR

SACRED DRAGON
PUBLISHING

Los Angeles, California - Sedona, Arizona

Copyright © 2021 Shaku Selvakumar

All rights reserved. No part of this book may be
reproduced in any form, except brief excerpts for
the purpose of review, without the expressed
permission of the publisher. and copyright owner.

Print ISBN: 978-1-7366793-5-7
Ebook ISBN: 978-1-7366793-6-4

Editing by Sacred Dragon Publishing
Creative Director: Francine Marie-Sheppard

First published by Sacred Dragon Publishing, Los Angeles, CA, December 2021
sacreddragonpublishing.com

Dedication

This book is dedicated to my parents, Parameshwari and Selvakumar, and my three daughters, Tanisha, Amaya, and Lila.

Every dream needs steady ground and inspired sky.

TABLE OF CONTENTS

Dedication iii

Preface vii

Retreat 1

Repair 25

Rejoice 55

Renew 89

Epilogue 121

Acknowledgments 125

About the Author 127

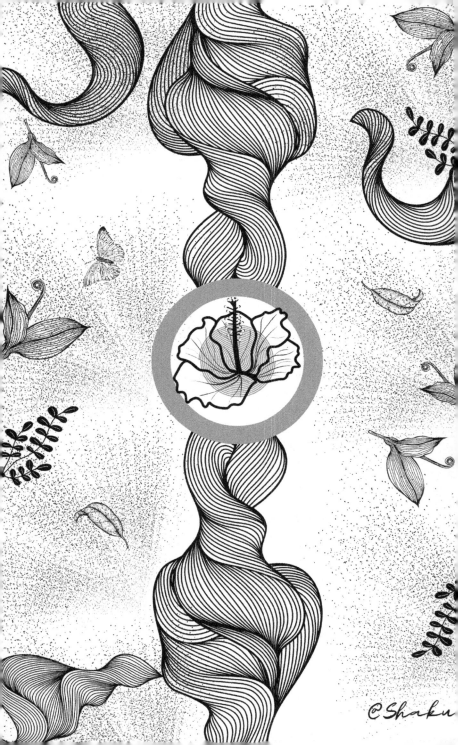

PREFACE

Within each seed lies a journey to be birthed.
And to each a journey as unique as a fingerprint.

Fingerprint

I started writing poetry in 2006 when a dear friend died suddenly in an accident. This was my first real tryst with the impersonal and impossible face of mortality. As I grappled with the loss and a sense of futility, I wrote my first poem, *The Flight of Doves,* from a place of existential angst. This awoke an inner voice I had not yet heard or shared. Once we discover a channel within, it becomes a powerful conduit that observes and informs. In the middle of a busy life and many roles, the larger questions of this existence sought me out.

Does my journey mean anything?

Whether healthy, sick, mother, father, elder, or youngster, rich, or poor, I saw that we share a oneness in our universal wish for love. We all seek visibility and fear loneliness and invisibility. To be alone and unloved is the harshest terrain to traverse. Yet, in its depths lies the wisdom that no one is unloved, none are unforgotten, and all are beloved souls.

As the inner world opens to this greater love, the outer world becomes an adventure where fear cannot cripple our stride.

This book is a collection of fifteen years of words strung together in my heart through love that have found their way onto the page. The river that flows inside starts dancing with the outside and what makes its way to the page is my offering back into the collective ocean of humanity.

To me, poetry is a portal. At the right time, at the right place, words unlock hidden memories and can provide a missing clue to an existential puzzle.

At the intersection of every moment lies choice. When we subscribe to the belief that life is lived only in a straight line from the past through the present towards the future, the opportunity for growth and change may lie dormant in an endless chain of reactive and fatalistic choices. But by understanding that we live cyclically through a flow of birth, death, and renewal—creation, maintenance, and destruction, we are not condemned to live in the auto-repeat of past choices. Instead, we can choose to see wisdom revealed in our suffering, in our humility born of failure, and in the nurture of nature. We can choose to relax our stranglehold on the need to control as a great act of courage.

Mistakes, mishaps, and missteps are heavy, but the beauty of life lies in the heart of its mystery. When pain and pleasure are both accepted, there is a sweet opening. The closed fist morphs into the open palm that invites grace and gratitude.

This book is tuned to the cycle of retreat, repair, rejoice, and renewal as I moved from endings to beginnings, failures to successes, exhaustion to restoration, emptiness to fullness, and arrived at exaltation and supplication. Through poetry, I found that I could address and redress, examine and reexamine, retreat, and greet what was awaiting my attention. It also permitted me to embrace every stage of the cycle. Through the writing, I found release and forgiveness. I recognized blame and shame. Through witnessing the sun rise and set, the moon wax and wane, and the seasons pass, I found that joy seeks no permission, only inner recognition.

Be Still My Heart is a living journey that has no beginning and no end. You can take a linear view from the first page to the next or turn to a random page and find what speaks to you.

The Flight of Doves

Send in the angels; he lived alone
Entombed before he left.

Send in the clowns, he wept unknown
This burden of mine I bear.

The flight of doves towards
The light set free
A spirit unchained by rewards
Of eternity.

The hunger inside
To be and see
Fortunes ebb and decide
The path of destiny.

Waves foam frothy white
Savage heart at which
Duty binds tight
Restless against the fight.

To each a heel of Achilles
Marked and crossed bright red
To love and please

But leave like a thief in the night.

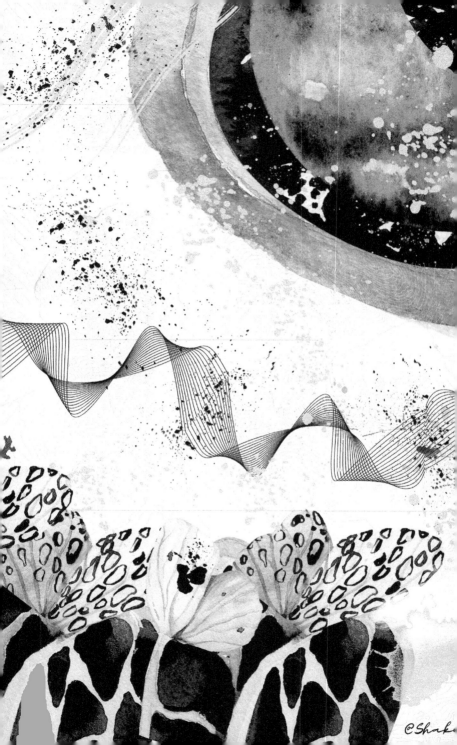

RETREAT

Teardrops are the waters of life
Flowing from the rivers of the heart.

Teardrops

Between the dance of the past and the present, the promise of change keeps us from falling completely apart. Sometimes change smashes into you and uproots your entire life. It leaves you at ground zero, gasping for air. Other times, you see change coming like a slow drip-feed of signs and omens. Yet, even if we can read the signs, most of us choose to ignore them and, like the ostrich, bury our head in the sand, hoping the view beneath the surface will protect us and keep us oblivious to the chaos churning above.

If you could peer into a crystal ball foretelling your fate or the fate of your children and their children, would you still want to live?

Knowing that pain, betrayal, fear, and sadness will wash upon your shore more frequently than days of sunshine and roses, would you still want to walk that path? What would you do when you couldn't recall the stone that you had cast so many years ago that had set in motion events that you could no longer control?

Though suffering is universal, and pain falls into every domain, the temptation to project it onto others through the twin sisters of blame and shame can feel insurmountable against the courage needed to end the misery and look within rather than without.

For me finding the courage to go within began with allowing space for retreat. It was here in the quiet of retreat that I could conserve my strength and stop myself from drowning in the sadness and despair that had pooled in the well of my grief. With the outside noise too much to bear and my heart and body unwilling to go on regardless of what my mind said, I sought solace in the quietude of simply knowing my grief. By resisting the temptation to pretend that everything was alright, I stepped out of rationalizing and compensating. In returning to the womb of solitude, my sorrow had safe passage to be seen, felt, heard, and released, so it did not take permanent residence in my heart.

Recall

I cannot remember anymore
What you said to me.

My heart empties like the river
Meeting the sea
Carrying little rocks
And holy life.
Mixing tears and fears
Churning sun-kissed places
And weather-worn faces.

To forgive,
I must first recall
What I once forgot.

Grief

i

Once the grief had run
its course,
water carving valleys
releasing its weight in
stone,
there was nothing
to give up
but the cost of
holding on
nothing left
but to be
free.

ii

Today i write
of everything dark
of shadows with teeth
of slime and grime
and claws and feet.

Today i descend
into the barren lands,
like Isis
and Nephthys
searching for
Osiris
into lands only
grief can follow.

iii

i want to know
how many times
a phoenix rises
before the ashes
are torn asunder
so scattered
far into the yonder
that there is nothing
left behind,
no feather
left to gather.

iv

There are parts of me that lie devastated,
like arid desert where endless sand stretches
wave upon wave,
roasted daily by the
merciless heat of the cruel sun.

i cannot outrun my regrets.
i cannot forsake my shame.

Both shadows follow me into daylight
into night.

v

Sometimes only the
torrent
that claims you
can clean you
and clear you.

Loss

i don't know how you can jump out of bed,
rush into the morning and race through
the day.

Today, i can't.

i don't know how you can stay eager and motivated,
no matter the news, no matter the views.

Today, i can't.

i don't know how you can plan for the future,
2021, 22, 23, 24.

Today, i can't.

Today my bones feel heavier than stone,
and my body feels worn.
My "must do's" and "should do's" are
gathering dust as I sit staring into the unknown
unable to even take a sip from my glass filled with
liquid.

My mind is a blur of competing voices, and
My heart is warped with the wire of hopeless.
My bed is my sea of imprisonment and sweet solace.
i dread my phone with its incessant notifications
of other people's success and the failure of the world.
i invite the small screen to carry me

into the forgetful space of an on-demand binge.
Thriller, yes
Comedy, no
Drama, yes
Horror, no
My fingers do the talking.

Don't tell me to step up or sit up,
stand up or show up.
Don't give me pithy phrases of can do's,
Of the best that is yet to come
Or the way to win the race.

The burden of loss trembles upon my soul.
Like a leaf that has been cast off its branch,
Like a bird that has lost its wing,
unable to now imagine the possibility of flight.
Sorrow is murky, a swamp that swallows.

Today, i can't
Tomorrow is a maybe.

The Kernel

there are days
gloomy ones
which come by
and take you
to faraway places
that you put off
visiting.

for the twin companions
of despair and despondency
are hard to forsake.
so dogged are they,
in their unwelcome
friendship.

but traversing the wilderness
is part of the map.
in the wallowing
in the swamp
in the dark terrains
of the damp,
there lies a kernel.

a kernel
of truth,
a clue to how
you came to be
and how
you can be free.

Heart Song

Where would your heart end and mine begin?
Is it in the valley of long-lost friends?
Or at the peak of treasured moments?
How does the thought of loss figure in?

When each day grinds into the next
Shredding the minutes into an inevitable past,
When i look up and say "remember when"
And you look at me, eyes slightly damp,
Thinking of the day before yesterday
A younger time,
When you wore courage like a worthy cape
And i held up hope like an impenetrable shield.

When our worlds first collided,
When we believed that heaven could be summoned,
And time could be held forever in a bottle
With three little words.

Liminal

what is this threshold,
between worlds
of the thinning veil,
flickering light
and transitioning of
life?

neither here nor there,
up nor down,
inside or outside,
between past and future.

during the great restructure
of beliefs and identity,
the walls fall and
all that is held within
rigid self breaks apart.
part by part.

dissolution of order,
of right and left,
correct and incorrect,
upper or middle,
greater or less,
profit or loss,
home or homeless,
neither above nor below,
we stand suspended
upside down.

this place untold
by prophecy,
of no guarantees,
of upheaval and reversal,
crushed in the cocoon
of transformation,
we swim on the cusp of
entry and exit,
of form and reform,
of chaos and miracles.
liminality.

Blame and Shame

The burden of both.
Like the worm
Burrowing
Deep in the heart,
A canker that spreads
Tearing us apart.

Both blame and shame
End with "me."

The Pyre of Change

i blocked it out
yesterday.
the grey skies
and the clouds
swollen with rain.
all that pain.
last night a friend
came over and we
walked after the sun
had set.

the light was dark
we talked late into the night
about survivors,
young ones
and not so young,
some older and the really old,
so old that memories were worn
frayed around the edges
like bridal silk that
had been insidiously
devoured by moths over time.

BE STILL MY HEART

this morning we prayed
for more strength
more grit
more patience
more persistence
more steel
forged from
centuries of waiting.

Enduring.

then we danced
for our daughters
and our sons,
feeling the earth
strengthening
our feet
and
take in
the bitter stench of
disappointment
despondence,
turning it
distilling it
into fuel,
because we will
not give up.

and once again
we will take
everything
unfair
unworthy
unkind
and burn
it on the
pyre
of
change.

Re(move)

i, who have left one house
after another,
am weary
of packing and unpacking,
of brown boxes and tape,
of scissors and waste.

i am tired of contracts
that bind me to your walls.

i, who have turned
house into home,
then home into house,
now want to leave the
paintings on the walls
and the books on the shelves.

i want to take the plants out
of the pots and root them
into the ground.

i want to stay here
for awhile
and catch my breath,
and let time and belonging
find each other
through the cracks
in my spirit
and weld it
together.

The Glass Slipper

The glass slipper was tight
But she heeded not the fit.

Wasting time that
Was hers to lose,
She now lies awake
Wondering where the hours flew.

Bitter taste of shortcuts and haste,
Echoes of arguments recycled again,
Apologies long forgotten
On silence and pain,
No glue from Bacchus or
Eros can adequately erase.

Turning to pumpkins
As midnight beckons,
Fairy tales and spells
Were meant to be broken.

The House of Belonging

She walked into the House of Belonging
Oblivious of any wrongdoing.

Stepping into cluttered rooms
Hearing echoes from childhood wombs,
Memories from teenage years
Brave planets orbited without fear.

So comfortable she was not shedding her skin
Hugging it tightly, she sat within.

For in seeking, you surely will find
Not always what you had in mind

She searched today in the House of Love.
The furniture was swept away.

She sat in the dark in the House of Faith
With nothing at hand but the hope of grace.

She picked up bricks in the House of Trust
For a strong foundation instead of fear.

She made friends in the House of Gray
Every strand had something to say,

For the journey inside crosses terrain unknown
A forked path, a blossoming tree,

She waits to see
She stays to see.

Just One Minute

A minute is the difference
between early and late.
A second is the difference
between life and death.
One word is the difference
between heaven and hell.
A world saved, swerved, or shattered
Giving hope or despair.
Life can be pared down to the bones,
Not by volumes of what was planned
But by a single decision, an act
By a minute, a second,
A word.

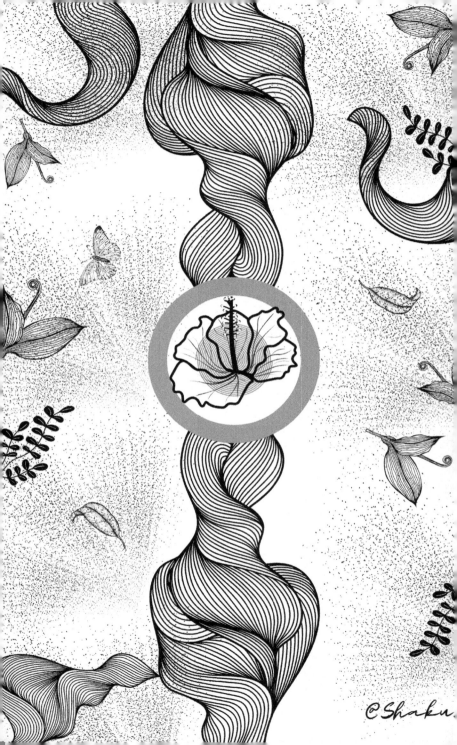

REPAIR

why do you believe…?

after all that you have seen
after all that you have heard
after all that you have learned
after all that you have experienced,

why do you believe others,
over yourself?

On the ledge

Arising from retreat and preparing to step back
into the world, there are moments when we are
dragging our feet and feeling disobedient, not
wanting to emerge fully from the protective space
of hibernation. As we are pulled towards something
that we are not ready to meet, this may be a time
to examine where life lacks luster or tiredness that
has robbed us of our inner vision.

For those tired of the accelerated pace of our world,
where everyone talks faster, acts immediately, and
hustling is some sort of admirable quality, the
reluctance to show up and engage fully with the
outside takes different forms. Sometimes it shows
up in the ways we subconsciously procrastinate
or self-sabotage by inviting the imposter in

to convince us that our dreams are much too grand. But reluctance is not always an act of self-deception. Sometimes it is the wisdom of hesitancy gained through a greater intelligence asking us to wait—asking us not to rush into realms we are not yet ready to inhabit.

Fatigue from the weight of our past and the numbing confusion of life in transition can quickly bring old patterns of self-sabotage to the surface. But what if the reluctance we feel is rooted in a deeper intuition around the importance of right timing? Perhaps it is signaling the need for a gradual transition out of overwhelming inertia of retreat into an awareness of nurturing rest and repair from our place of hibernation. All great movements, all inspired creations, were birthed in the cauldron of opposition and fluctuation. Ideation and innovation often spring from the throes of transition.

"Re" pair is to pair again by paring off unwanted baggage and pairing anew with the wisdom of your soul. Instead of running away or hiding, we use resistance to find a new path to a greater self. As we work through winter's gestation, the ground beneath is quiet, preparing for spring just as we remain quiet while preparing to emerge.

The Spectrum

Laugh with the world but don't hide your tears.
You will be surprised how many can understand
sorrow.

Ask for what you want but don't hinge your happiness
on it.
Sometimes not getting what you want
Could lead you to what you need.

There are no winners or losers.
A loss today can turn out to be a win tomorrow,
Just like something can begin only at the end.

No one knows your shoes like you do
Wear them well. Wear them out.
Leave your footprints. Nobody wants invisibility.

Love with generosity, with compassion.
Don't be a miser. All that hoarding leads to
unhappiness.

Don't be afraid of yes. Don't be hesitant about no.
Nostalgia is a mind-altering drug that keeps you stuck
in the past.

Laugh; it's contagious.
Cry, it unlocks the reserved pain.

Learn, never stop.
Listen, it's at the heart of connection.
Practice wonder.
Magic is the flower that blooms for a day.

Treasure your body. Don't curse it or abuse it.
You need it for the journey.

In your mind, you can be a ruler, a soldier, a beggar,
or a thief.
Control is an illusion. A strength can be a weakness.

So, make peace with paradox, with polarities and
ambiguities.
Take the life walk without desperation, judgment, or
impatience.

We may start with nothing.
We may leave with nothing.
But a game well played could mean something.

Midnight

i was always afraid of the dark
Until one midnight alone, I sat
Under the canopy of the silent sky.
In the company of the winking stars,
And the wind, he whispered in my ear
Secrets only i could hear
Stay still and feel, let go and let be
You are part of me, even as you breathe.

Old Friends

Old friends meet in the middle of "remember whens."

When the light was pure and hearts were whole
Barely bruised, soft, and tender,
When possibilities were boundless
Chariots awaited, dreams were daring,
Wearing rose-colored glasses, skipping on cloud nine,
When youth feared nothing
Nothing at all.

Old friends travel the years of distance,
Recounting the time when children grew up,
Recalling the instances when the heart shattered
Falling on the floor, a million pieces,
Then bending down to pick up the fragments
And slowly pieced together again.

Old friends glance at each other's faces
At creases that have appeared
Where once was unlined skin,
At the remnants of who they were
Lingering in the eyes,
Touching the smile and caressing the lips
The face that was once brash, defiant
Now accepting of the winds of change.

Old friends exchange bursts of information,
Retelling old stories as they reinvent themselves,
Toggling between past and present,
Sometimes laughing at their blinkered selves.
Their discussions now richer
With an adjusted view into the future,
Filling every crevice in the conversation
Followed by pauses of understanding,
Nodding when no word is needed,
A hand reaching out during moments of silence.

Old friends say goodbye
Their confessions intact,
Burdens slightly lightened
Some advice exchanged.
This time was a respite,
But their other world breaks through
Text messages and phone calls.
They stand up and hug,
Promising to stay in touch
To make plans to meet soon.
Life is too short, they say
For friends to stay away.

Role Call

I have found that it is not enough
To think you can sing
To think you can write
To think you can create
To think you can change.
If you are left to only thoughts
There would be only wind,
Thunder and sound
And never any rain.

That mountains will always
Stand in your path
More formidable from the distance,
That other voices will always
Have their say,
And logic will usually
Rule the day.

I have seen courage in action
Of a little seed fumbling underground
Finding its way
To send one green shoot tentatively
Seeking the sun,
Knowing that there was no guarantee
Or safety above ground.

How long can you incubate
Needing the comfort of the umbilical cord,
Or the prophecy of a crystal ball?

Unless you step out of thoughts
To walk out of the door,
You will never know the temperature outside,
Or that the storm that had to be faced
Was more sound than fury.

You will never know
That shoes were meant to get dirty,
That hands were meant to get calloused,
That your heart was built to handle pain.

With the power of every little step,
Your feet that walked the many miles
Sometimes questioning the compass
Many times, questioning yourself,
Would increase your appetite for risk
Would flex the muscle of the spirit
Would build your stamina,
Strengthening the core
To remember that all will cross the finishing line.

But life is not an endurance race,
A pageant, or a contest
About whom reaches first, middle, or last,
Or whose name graced the Hall of Fame.
It is about making peace
With your recollection
Of how you finally cast yourself.

Untether

don't go gently into the night
where your failures stare at you
with sharpened teeth.
don't pretend with glass in hand
that success is your middle name,
that you are incapable of defeat.
what lies you tell?
what lies beneath
late at night,
fails to hold
in the daylight?
run far; run fast,
that doesn't work either.
stay rocking in the past,
that will not last.
don't believe another's
airbrushed picture,
swim through it
the heavy sludge.
As you fall in pieces
to find peace,
face the war.
for to save,
you must sacrifice.
to find redemption,
swim in the valley
of regrets.

BE STILL MY HEART

seek salvation
by letting go of
shame.
the other half,
the mid-point,
the muddling middle,
the midheaven
unraveled, unwrapping,
untethered, unveiling,
unique, uniting,
is
all part of the
universe.

Maps

There is a place
Where memories stay tender,
Like newly birthed leaves
Unfurling in hope and surrender,

Where the twilight Sun lingers longer
Holding heat undercover,
When the world is coated in hues of
Of pink and some lavender.

We are brave again,
Letting go of careworn maps drawn by another
Shedding outworn suffocating skin
Weeding out the hauntings of sorrow and sin.

This time of dreaming
Snapping out of slumber,
Reunited with the one voice
Unscripted and unhindered.

Clouds

Clouds pass by, gathering
Scattering, rehearsing, rehashing,
Carrying rain like sorrow withheld,
Growing heavy, darkening overhead.
Before armies meet on the battlefield,
Long is the night of restless dreams
Kingdoms won; treaties signed.
Promises lost, people in haste.
Clouds drift by, dimming the sun
Pretending to stay but moving again
Soft shapeshifters, Heaven's wanderers.
Where do you go? who do you love?

No

"No" is absolute.
It stands alone,
Not asking for a companion
Nor giving an explanation.
No is your backbone
Straightening your stoop
Fixing your neck
Squaring your shoulder.
Use it wisely.
Combine it with grace
It speaks to boundaries that get often eroded.
Use it sparingly but without regret.
No is not a mantra.
No is not Maybe.
No gives you pause for breath.
No is the space in between.
No speaks to the importance of Enough.
No is the positive within the negative
Providing an end
So the new can begin.
No lets you say Yes
When the time is right
Without hesitation
Without resentment.

Fare Well

Would you ask why the sun sets,
Or question the moon
On her disappearance,
Or expect the hibiscus
To bloom but not wilt,
Or save every fallen swift?
The betrayal of change
The constant cycle,
How we live
The way we love,
How we farewell.

A Bouquet of Ideas

Don't hoard ideas,
Else they die.
Share them.
Give them the spotlight.
Some will take flight
Some will not.
Some will give credit
Many will not.
How does it matter?
Where soil is fertile,
Flowers bloom in abundance.

The Siren Song

There is a siren within each of us.
The song that only you can hear.
Even when you pretend to be deaf,
Even if you stick your head in the sand,
there is a call.

You will find a way to answer it.
This is how we find ourselves in
foreign places with unfamiliar faces.

Here you settle down,
you find your new people.
You raise your family,
and you send out roots.
If the soil is fertile,
it takes hold and the flowers
bloom fragrant and sweet.

If there is too much nostalgia,
the fruit is bitter.
Somewhere there is a thread
of shoulda, coulda, woulda.
Somewhere there is a parallel path
of a different life of the road not taken.

The fallacy lies in the belief
that we somehow missed the call
to act in the perfect story
where everything adds up,
the sun shines on cue,
the rain falls and only just so,
the storm is for background effect,
and lightning never strikes.

What if everything that has brought you here,
right up to this very moment
was all that you had to go through?

what if,
your mistakes,
your detours,
your blunders,
your victories,
your right turns,
your high fives,
your rejections,
your humiliations,
your successes,
your laughter,
your tears,
your arrivals,
your departures,
your hellos,
your goodbyes,
your infatuations,

your pain,
your gain,
your vanity,
your insanity,

were the ingredients that your soul
needed to understand where you would go from here?

What if we took responsibility for this place
instead of casting doubt and finding blame?

And how we would take our life forward
instead of playing the usual game?

The Clue

The wonder of any day lies in unearthing some treasure
Because you took time to follow a clue.
Not all treasures are created equal,
Some lead to a vocation,
Some lead to an idea or a long-lost friend,
Some lead to the person you end up saying "I do" to,
Some lead to words, spoken or written, that fill your Heart.

With the possibility of the impossible
Following the rabbit down the hole is what Alice did first.
She then grew shorter, taller,
and later it was nearly "off with her head."
But if you hold back, and you stay still,
If you refuse to stand up, to place foot one in front of the other,
The act of being muted will fester inside,
Like Bilbo middle-aged, safe in the Shire
With Constance by his side and comfort only money can buy,
Who still ventured outside
Understanding that age is irrelevant.

Even if you were wrong, you still picked up a fight
Sometimes taking a left when it did not feel right.

Sometimes the trip outside may need backpacks,
water, and a compass.
Sometimes the journey is within, and the excavation
needs only a flashlight.
When fears cast long shadows like clawing Orcs with
fierce sharpened teeth,
When doubts and ridicule threaten to open old
wounds,
When the mocking face of failure morphs with
success,
Each knowing that the other is just a play of light.

One day a King the next day with no clothes.
What else can you do but to follow the clue
With no map or a spot marked X,
For the treasure that you find may not be gold coins
But richness that will change your life.

Ask

All you must do is ask, they said.
But I find I rarely ask.
Draw a picture then, they said;
Ahh, but it changes even before I start.

Truth be told, I don't want to ask.
I want to be surprised,
To unlock clues, fall into mystery.

Would I have known to ask for you?
Would I have seen the world unfold
In ways that I could never behold,
When I was ten or twenty
or even now?

The Cup

Every glass that is half empty
contains a promise that was never fulfilled.
And every glass that is half full
promises magic that can never be emptied.

The Muse

i

Ask anyone
Serious about their craft,
Nothing happens overnight.
A price must be paid.
There is no lottery
Spiraling you to fame.
Ask anyone
Who taps the muse,
A fleeting touch
A spark
A forgotten note,
Ask anyone
Who showed up for years,
Playing till dawn
Ignoring the whispers
Questioning their talent.
Ask anyone
Who worries about mediocrity,
Wearing heart on sleeve
About being left to wallow
Like a weed, untended, ignored.
Ask anyone
Fearing the day
That nothing will follow,
A blank page
With naught to offer,

Or a canvas
Of empty,
Of feet that fail,
Voice that falters,
Hands that fumble,
Memory that lapses,
Leaving fragments of fear.
Ask anyone
Who has had one glimpse
Of Creation,
Who has experienced
Singular connection,
Manna from heaven
Leaving doubt by the wayside
And logic at the wake.
Ask anyone
Who knows all of the above,
They will tell you
If they had to choose once more
At the road that forked
Between highway and hell,
They would still choose the muse
All over again.

ii

If i stare at this page long enough
Like old friends who went away,
Long lost words will eventually appear
From hidden recesses, confined spaces,

Places forgotten in the mansion of memory
They rush forward like a dam released
And i have to tell them,
"Please stand in line so I can sort you out."

Like finding pieces of a jigsaw puzzle,
Trying to understand
What needs to be said first
And who goes next.

Some i file away for another day.
These are fragments without head or tail,
Just a struggling thought that flickers with hope
But needs so much more to flesh it out.

i jot it down somewhere hoping
i will be able to greet them at a later time.
Some i am not ready to meet.
These are not primed for the light of day
For scrutiny or candor or further investigation.
These must wait, marinating in their juices,
Like raisins for a rum cake,
And carefully stored away.
Then there are thoughts that flow with grace
Flying fluid, faster through fingers,
Racing through the head,
Speaking through the heart,

They fumble for a bit trying
To match words with wit,
Then they rush by leaving you
Breathless as you sit back
Trying to read what you just wrote.

Did that make sense?
Did it make the cut?
Was it all only in my head?

But if I don't stare long enough
At the paper or the screen,
If I don't show up,
If I push it away,
Making time instead for the mundane
Magic never happens.

It flickers out like fireflies
Dead before daylight,
Leaving me wandering and
Wondering about something
I cannot remember,
Something I shouldn't forget.

REJOICE

On the barest branches of the redbud tree,
Stripped dry by winter's harsh breath
Before the advent of tender green shoots,
Little pink buds courageously appeared,
Declaring the rebirth of life
The bee, butterfly, bird, and beast found
Its song again.

The Redbud Tree

For the longest time, I thought that I was a city girl. I loved the hustle and bustle of buildings and people, cars, and planes. This was the heart of action and reaction.

Then, in 2008, I found myself in a new home surrounded by live oak, cedar, and crepe myrtle trees. Leaves from redbud trees mingled with bougainvillea vines. I watched the esperanza plants revive every summer after being cut down the previous winter. Every year, I wondered if the hibiscus flowers would return. Would the fig, the pomegranate, the lemon, and the peach trees bear fruit?

In this place, I saw the way nature follows the sun as it crosses the sky and comes to stillness under the moon, the way no two sunsets were alike, and the way spring made everyone instantly happy.

I found out how deer may be timid and tentative but equally brave and beautiful. I learned that male cardinals seeking the magical other are fascinated by their appearance and smash into glass windows time and time again. I watched the swans, so awkward on land, gracefully glide across the water and the way the roadrunner left offerings of wood and bark at my patio door.

I saw how the hawk soars, rising high, then swoops down in a flash to grab a scurrying mouse. Turkey vultures that I had once feared now looked magnificent drying their wings in the midday sun. Even the deadly coral snake slithering across my path reminded me it was only making progress along its path.

The natural world is a source of endless nourishment to me. It is a constant teacher and patient healer. From the time we are born, we are part of our natural cycle of appearing, disappearing, and reappearing.

Emerging from our own cycle of hibernation, we can rejoice in the abundant inspiration of growth and renewal that flows naturally in the spring. Even after a deadly forest fire, devastating flooding, or a snow apocalypse, life is re-infused with intelligence. Day follows night; spring follows winter. But light cannot find its way to us if the door is shut, the curtains are drawn, and the windows are sealed. So often, we turn away, pushing back on hope because the world and its ailments seem like an unending litany of woes rather than opening to the possibility of joy beyond our closed windows and shut doors.

Our smallness and sense of insignificance create a falsely insurmountable barrier that remains until we bravely look upon the light of day and see the life bursting forth from the warmth of the sun.

This section of poetry is closest to my heart. Whether I have lain in retreat or sat in repair, it is my conversations in the natural world that have reconnected me with the wisdom of the world and the source of my joy.

Cactus

We grow in the night
When nobody's looking.
Away from the harsh glare
As the frantic work of the day
Starts seeping in,
When daydreams coalesce with nightmares
And wheat is sifted from the chaff,
Even a cactus
Thorny and defensive,
Growing in the wilderness,
Water so scarce,
Love so bare,
Will still send her best offering,
A yellow bloom
Without fail, every Spring,
As if to say
I will take what I find
And turn it to gold.
I am Alchemy.
In heat or cold,
I will not fold.

Hibiscus

i

The generosity of the yellow hibiscus
with a red center
To bloom at sunrise,
to give the world everything
without holding back,
And at sunset to let beauty go.

ii

Deeply red,
She is the sacred cup of life and longing,
Of blood, birth, and beckoning,
The chalice of creation and [re]creation.

iii

The work of the hibiscus is to unfold
Into its finest hour,
Opening for light
And closing at night.

iv

Unfettered
Unsullied
She blooms
Unabashedly,
An answer only to
Life's longings.
An ode to
Beauty
Spirit
Glorious
Basking
In the light,
Claiming her brief
Her single day
Under the Sun.

v

Soft, tender, and radiant,
These violet hues of
Unearthly beauty
Are a symbol of devotion
And humble perfection,
As fleeting as the moment
Like miracles that leave
A lasting fragrance,
The Rose of Sharon
revives after being dormant.

Winter of The Redbud Tree

The redbud tree
Stands bare of her heart-shaped
Leaves.
Her clothes lie
Scattered
Littering the ground.
In the darkest night
The cold
Creeps in,
Covering
Her feet
Her naked limbs
Her balding crown.
So it has begun again,
This time of necessary
Fall,
This time of
Letting go,
This time of
Standing still,
Of stressful weathering
Contracting and retreating,
This place of vigil.

She does not know what this winter
will bring,
If her roots will hold ground,
If her body will stand strong,
As the wind pushes her around,
As the water sends
shivers of ice
up her spine.
While the light shies away
behind the grey,
The redbud tree Stands bare of leaves,
Facing another winter
Alone
More beautiful
in her sanguine
vulnerability
Than attired in her
verdant
best.

Mountains and Streams

I sit here in front of mountains unmoving
Tall and imposing
Wondering how to bring that stillness inside me.

Rock of ages
Witness to every war that wages,
Bearing the weight of fickle seasons
Where trees grow, shed, and drop,
Where rain falls, sometimes softly,
Sometimes crashing, clashing
With the morphing skies above,
Stubborn, holding firm to the ground
Not easily undone.

I see streams froth and foam at your foothills
Helpless against will or weather,
So easily roused by the air of fury
Ranting, always rushing,
Surging, restless, brimming, brewing
Evaporated by heat, humbled by cold,
Carrying life that must swim along
Always forward, sometimes crashing against stone
That stand up without warning like sentries
To test the resolve of the journey by water.
Even as it looms, the steep waterfall,
She cannot stop
Or retrace her steps.

I need them both,
The mountain to ground my feet
To stay my mind
To hold my fears
To pass the strength of infinite time
To endure the fierce, the feeble
To remember the ascent is entwined
With descent,
The stream to manage the flow
To gather the wisdom of the many
To be fluid, to take the plunge
Embrace each change
To harness the wind
Reflect the sun
To absorb the rain
Grow the grain
To quench the thirst
Clean the scars,
To take the journey
As separate strands
But forsworn to one tapestry.

Twilight

I saw the Sun before he left.
He said, "Look up above, my friend
Tell me what you think
Of this evening's masterpiece.
I picked up my brush.
I threw in some orange,
Some blue, some red.
I borrowed some clouds
A layer here, a puff there.
The sky stayed still.
She lets me play.
She knows I hate to go away.
Those days when I stay up too late,
The Moon gets impatient.
She steps in, and for a brief moment,
Like Yin and Yang,
We share this space."

I stare at the shimmering farewell,
At colors, hues, sheen, and blues
This coda of brilliance,
Radiance,
Iridescence.
I tried to take a picture
To prove to you that Heaven exists.
But I know that nothing man-made
No words, verse, chant, or hymn
No Pantone shade, no palette, no lens
Can capture the sight
Of the glorious passing of another fleeting day.

Rain Lily

Where did you come from?
Little white one
Seeking your place, your face to the Sun,
Untended, unloved, swept in by the rain,
Nature's understudy to the favored bluebonnet,
Sprouting out of cracks in pavements
Tender roots taking hold against stone,
Standing strong next to Heaven's own roses,
Neglected, children of the slum
To stay for a while and leave unnoticed,
Like love that grows in unexpected places.
You are no less, oh wild, pale beauty
A touch of grace, to each their fate
Demeter's forgotten daughter,
You are Persephone's sweet, wistful laughter.

Kotagiri

Somewhere between earth and heaven
Exist scalloped hills of tea gardens
Circled by spiraling narrow pathways.
Eucalyptus sharply clears the air.
Blooms of color brighten the fringes.
Light shines only softly here.
Rain mists the land throughout the year.
Indecisive fog plays hide and seek
Rising slowly, then drifting without warning
Covering every mountain peak.

A changeling knowing not what she seeks
Somewhere between silence and sound.
The bison wanders slowly in no hurry to get around.
Birds want to gently intrude,
Even the harsh crow tries to fit in here.
A panther, a tiger may be spotted at night.

As boundaries merge into the wild unknown
Somewhere between cool and cold
The Sun disappears and reappears like a whimsical child.

Tea pickers glide silently through rows of leaves
Unfazed by the rain, the chill, they have bags to fill.
No highways can be seen over here.
Narrow single-lane roads snake up every
mountainside.
Cars honk to announce presence, not impatience.
School children walk home together.

Somewhere retreat and reprieve heal
Sore eyes and heart tired by the frenzied city.
Time is measured by cups of tea.
Through these verdant ancient hills
A fragile partnership exists.
Man may eke his livelihood on natural terrain
But here, supremacy is not an option.

March Moon

I saw the March moon last night
Rise to find her place in the sky,
Brilliant, powerful
Flooding the rooms with light
And breaching the inner city.

Invading the shifting terrains of sleep,
Diving into the waters of the subconscious,
Searching for sunken forgotten treasures,
She stayed in full splendor through the night.
Not inclined to leave or fade away,
Lingering well past dawn
Even when the sun was clearly in sight,
Turning to a softer golden hue
From her usual glistening white,
Sitting in the house of scales
La Luna speaks of balance,
Self-illumination.

What part of you have you hidden away?
What part of you have you given away,
What lies beneath your calm exterior?
What risks are you afraid to take?
Where are those demons safely stored?
What clips your wings and fights your flight?

I saw the Full Sap Moon last night
Calling me to forgotten places,
Signaling the end of winter,
Heralding the return of robins
And the emergent Spring.
When the ice thaws slowly
And the earthworms appear
Telling me to befriend the mystery,
Be patient with the uncertain
To face the darkness and the fear,
To find some solace despite the madness,
To seek the mystery behind the shadows,
To transform,
To reinvent,
To remember when to disappear,
And to reappear again.

Nature Therapy

Dear one,
When you sit outside as the light begins to melt
Just before the colors run riot in the sky,
Preoccupied with so many questions in your head
About emails unanswered
Or dishes piled up,
About what she said or what he meant
Absorbed with the world inside your head,
Did you see the butterfly kiss the redbud tree,
Or the spider move slowly across translucent skein
Shimmering in the evening light?
Did you notice the cardinals play a game of tag,
Or your dog nibbling patiently at a bone?
Did you hear the rustle of the leaves
Gently swaying in the breeze?
Did you look at the small shoots arising already
Signaling that March is here?
Did you hear the call of the chickadee
Pointing out that night is near?
Did you miss the sunny Carolina Jessamine
Bloom and grow, grateful for the absence of snow?
What else did you miss, my dearest friend?
As you sat in silence unmoved by beauty
Lost in your reverie, immersed in self-pity
Petulant, pushing aside natural therapy
Like a beggar seeking alms in the land of plenty.

Heron

In my knowing
That what lies ahead
Is worth the wait,
Like the heron
In her state of Grace,
Like the hermit in tree pose
Uncluttered by the chaos
Of others
Still
In
Active
Awareness.

Passiflora Incarnata

I am the purple
passionflower
That blooms in your light
And dies at night.
I am the red hibiscus
That unfolds for
just one sight.
I am the heart that sees
You are everywhere.
You are the painter,
I am your palette.
You are the poet,
I am unstrung letters.
You are the witness,
I am the writer, the director,
I am the actor; I am the act.

Dragonfly

Yesterday
The iridescent dragonfly
In electric metallic blue,
Found her way to me,

A gentle wisp, whirring,
Appearing, disappearing.

She stayed with me as I walked
Amongst green and grass,
Concrete and car.

Yesterday I carried her lightness
Of form and [re]form, of
Member and re-member
As I recalled the magic of
The subtle, the small
The significant,

To be able to dance on water
And waltz with the wind.
Each a key to portals
Unknown,
Unseen.

Beloved

I hold on to You
like the sand waits for the waves,
like the waves that toss
restless for the moon,
like the moon that
yearns for the advent of night,
like the night that
is swallowed by the light,
and the day is once again cast away.
I pray to You and
hear my voice echo into
emptiness,
yet the sound fills my thirsty heart
like the rain swallowed
by land that is parched,
like the earth that
gives back green and color,
and the tree that
yields the sacred flower.

Listen

i

They say that the Beloved takes
On many forms.
You don't know what you
Need to hear until
You really listen.

The earnest heart,
The stable heart,
And the eager ear
Is often blessed
With wisdom
Found in unexpected
Places,
In the form of unforeseen
Grace.

ii

Ask
then
Listen.

Not forgotten.
Not forsaken.

For the closed
Heart and the
Clenched fist
Cannot feel
The caress of
The feather,
Or the
Whisper
In the
Wind.

S(i)lence

a journey into the inner realm
where the sounds dissolve
and the chaos of the "I"
dissipates,
presence and prescience
changing the present
the past, the future.

floating up from the murkiness below
the treasure of truth emerges from the
waters of stillness,
freed and no longer silenced.
sight seeks clarity,
sounds dissipate, noise filtered out,
listening to
the steady beating of the heart,
to the wisdom carried in the breath,
finding at last the stream
where all souls flow.
silence,
the inner lens
focused on the lower case "i".

Bells

The path meanders...
sometimes a fork
can cut like a knife,
and the clouds can
obscure the sun,
and the rain
falls gently
on the pain.
then I find you
in the pause,
and You remind me
through the silence
where the bells are
ringing
and...
I hear the angels.
I hear them
singing.

Shakti

I tattooed her name just above my left breast.
As the needle went up and down, breaking skin,
touching blood,
creating an outline
Inking space that
was once empty,
and a promise was solemnly made.

Shringara

What sweetness is this?

the way the
light shimmers,
my heartbreaking
into song.

i take a picture
of this moment
nestled in joyful
abundance,
to hold it in
my kaleidoscope
of memories.

the radiance of
the world
as it beats for
every life,
pulsing, bursting
into daily
creation.

golden nectar
flowing through
vital pathways,
then retreating,
into daily
dissolution.

nothing too
small,
no one
unnecessary.

Gr(ace)

i

as soft as a feather
as tender as a whisper
as sweet as a newborn's grip
as subtle as gentle moonlight,
a fortunate reprieve,
an exemplary intervention,
an ordinary miracle,
the Ace of Cups
the Holy Grail
the hand that reaches
out from behind the clouds,
the heart that overflows
with incoherent, incredible
language.
to recognize Grace is the
first step to invite more
benediction.
a grant, a bequest,
always unexpected,
a holy favor, sanctification and
protection,
Grace is divine goodwill.

ii

I stepped off one path and found I had to pave another.
Some days I have to take three steps back,
Reverse slightly and take the detour.
Then I retreat
And wonder what will become of me.
Some days I gasp in awe
With what a single turn can unfold.
The vital scenery, the possibilities
I find myself in a dialog directly with life's mystery.
All dots seem to connect instantly.
These days I hold on with tenacity.
These days of singular grace and generosity
Given casually,
Benediction in exchange for acceptance
And stubborn persistence.

RENEW

Take today's blank
page and paint it with
the colors of
renewed vision.

Just like the dawn
steps softly onto the
stage every morning
as the traces of the
darkest night slip
away.

Renewed Vision

There are two calls we attune to every day. One is the call to serve our ego, and the other is to serve our soul.

The call of our ego is usually the loudest and most familiar. It starts with "I" and continues with either "want," "need," or "must" or "should." When we respond to the ego's call, we immediately don our armor and go into battle. For life feels like a battlefield, peppered with phrases like "winning," "losing," "hustling," "competing," and "comparing." It is a never-ending merry-go-round. Sometimes, we are the horse rider; sometimes, we envy the horse rider.

The other softer call is to serve our soul. This call starts with the small "i" and is always a request—an invitation for illumination to enter. From a place of humility that pleads "i don't know" or "please help me" or "show me," we open the door of co-creating with the unseen and the magical.

To become "new" is to shed the cynicism of "what is the use" and "what is the point." It starts with clearing the old lens and summoning the courage of a grander vision. We are called to empty and step into vulnerability. My favorite metaphor for this stage of renewal is the oak tree at the onset of summer. As summer approaches and temperatures rise, the oak trees respond by growing a full crown of leaves ready to provide shade for all in need. Renewal brings with it a mighty intention to expand into fullness and, through that abundance, share and be open to the greater good.

In renewal lies the inner reconciliation to uphold the promises made while in hibernation, remembering to constantly move forward in the present instead of backward through the past. By being vigilant in abandoning old unhealthy language and outdated narratives, we rewire and reprogram our actions.

Renewal is a daily mindset. Awakening to a new day gives us another opportunity to see the world from a new lens. It is the ongoing hope that by committing to the bigger arc of our lives, we can elevate our perspective and move out of the fatalistic prison of a smaller life.

Life Story

Own your story, or
others will make one up for you.
Own your history,
your mistakes, your triumphs.
As flawed as we are, the way to forge
forward is to make peace with the past.

Define your success.
Don't fret about approval.
Forgive yourself. Forgive others.
Say goodbye to the gossip,
the grudge and the judge.

There is an invisible ledger
that keeps the tally.
You cannot rewind time.
You cannot gamble with health.
You can keep finding higher ground.
You can mend fences.
You can tear down walls.
You can strengthen connections.

Life can take us deeper into division,
faster into our neuroses or
higher into the service of the heart.

Hold on to your freedom.
Use your influence wisely.
You can be the problem.
You can find the solution.
You can be caught in the chaos.
Or you can be strong at the core.

You have the right to choose.
You have the right to voice.
You have the power.
You have the choice.

There is truth in the ordinary.
There is beauty in duty.
If the ground is strong,
then the flight withstands the storms.
The mystery of our life is
what brings us back to the magic of living.

Reborn

These are days when
All that is known
All that is understood
All that is seen
All that is lived
Lie behind the filter
Of my hubris.
As I pull at the threads of my
conditioning,
The lens of my unseeing,
As I slowly untangle,
the knots first get tighter.
Not this.
Not that.
Not here.
Not there.

I become stranger,
Estranged,
A stranger to myself.

First, there are questions
And earnest questioning.
Yearning to bypass
To stay in the past.
Talking to ghosts
Of previous hauntings,
Resistance is rooted
In ancient voices as
they are slowly discovered
And tediously uprooted.

As all lies unravel,
As all lies unraveled,
The truth lies naked,
Reborn from the fire
An offering at the altar
Of departure and arrival.

A Love Letter

Yesterday I kept love
a secret from myself,
Stifling it in big
small-and-tiny ways,
Holding back,
rehearsing,
reviewing words.

Yesterday I worried about my own
vulnerability,
wondering about reception
scared about rejection,
focusing on perfection.

Yesterday I felt unworthy
about the gifts I carried
needing clear validation,
seeking constant approval,
wanting reciprocal participation,
till I found that Time had altered
its face,
till I realized that it had
accelerated its pace,
till I understood the futility of
hoarding my name,
till I knew that we were all the same.

Today is now,
it is my every day.
Take whatever I have to give.
Take whatever I have to say.
The guards are leaving the
cautious mind
and the gated heart.
Love is the contagious fire
transmitted without barriers,
sensing everything
fearing nothing
unwilling to barter
brimming with potential.

Today I kneel in prayer
with the intention
of allowing change,
in sweet surrender
so that I may never be the same.

The Tribe

i

For so many years I spoke fluently
The language of other tribes.
Though I moved in these places
With the greatest of ease,
Inside the imposter couldn't breathe.
To infiltrate and remain in disguise
Is to narrate a story that is not yours.

As time continues to flow,
The lines start blurring,
And the role that is played
Is the hero's foil.
Never to step into the spotlight,
Always the butler,
Never the knight.
So many archetypes in the arena; they fight,
Pick me; I am a martyr, the humble servant.
I always say yes when I want to say no.
No pick me, I am a rebel.
Oh poor me, cries the sad victim.
Nurture me, I am the child.
Always and forever, the mother vows.
Rescue me, the princess begs.
So long I have waited in a tower so tall
My godmother hasn't turned up,
My hero is late.

Don't waste time, the siren says.
Turn on the charm,
You will be nothing when you turn gray.
You are always wrong; the critic is vehement.
I am going to make you pay, the interrogator warns.
You will be punished, the priest intones.
Let it always be about me, the narcissist demands.

The voices grow louder
A continuous monologue.
Embittered, they parry
They heckle, prod and flounder,
Till you call them out by name
Find their fears and fight their foes.
When you are ready
For your own homecoming
Where familiarity
Is not contempt,
Then you will hear the
Call of your tribe,
Faint at first
And growing louder.
The ones who live on the edges
Voyagers and Pathfinders
They hear your words
And speak your language
Though not of your blood
But of your spirit.

ii

You want to hang out with sincerity.
You want to sit next to kindness.
You want to have a drink with goofy.
You want to cuddle up with joy.
You appreciate patience.
You recognize generosity.

This is the happiness of getting older,
Like cleaning your closet of sizes that
No longer fit.

Bridgebuilders

The story goes that
When you are young,
You must search for the ladder.
Your education is first geared
To find the bottom rung
When you graduate, cap and gown
Thrown asunder, clutching a piece of paper
That says you now hold the key
To take the first step.
The first step is not the hardest here
You run towards it, a little afraid
But it feels like you have finally
Found a clue to what
Will keep you busy
For a long time in your life.

Now you are part of the ladder
And as you start the climb
There are so many goals to reach.
You now meet the others
The race begins.
Who will climb the highest?
Who will climb the fastest?
Who was the youngest?
Who was most promising?
Who was the smartest?
So many superlatives
So many opinions, perceptions

And marked preferences
Tagged, and you are it.

Some will lose hope with the climb
Content to stay on the middle rung.
Some will rise with each step up
As the atmosphere thins.
The perks, first class,
A corner office,
A coveted parking spot,
The ladder holds them in its thrall
And identity is found in a business card.

But stories always have a twist.
The harder you hold on,
The longer you stay,
The more you enjoy us vs them,
The less time you have to
Contemplate your descent,
Unless you found a way
And you understood
That a ladder is one way
Only when propped up.
But placed flat on the ground,
It shifts from Me to We,
It encourages connection,
It becomes a path,
It becomes a bridge.

The Ordinary

Give me the ordinary day
With its quiet, steady light.

Give me the steam that rises from
The kettle whistling on the stove.

Give me the morning walk as the
Dog tugs at her leash
Wanting to chase the
Squirrel scampering around.

Give me the grocery run and the community
At the farmer's market.

Give me the laughter of a child carried by
The wind as I plant a sapling in rich soil.

Give me the dishes that need to be unloaded,
Or the laundry that has to be neatly folded.

Give me the boring and the sturdy,
The stable and the safe.

I don't need the drama or the
Excitement.
I am done with the dizzying high
And the rollercoaster lows.

Give me the sweet, quiet of the fan
Slowly revolving.

The even hum of an ordinary day.

2020

Last night I dreamed
of a thousand steps
Rising and falling
Pulling me down
Then taking me higher.

What was expected was
swallowed by the
unexpected,
Reshaped
Remodeled
Reversed
Irreversible.

I opened a window
that turned into an open door
Carrying my name
Carrying all our names.

By stepping in,
I stepped out.
Wearing a mask outside,
I removed the one inside.

Last night I dreamed of
a thousand eyes
and a million I's
Stripping me down
Facing my fears.
Last night I dreamed about
being grounded,
But not cornered,
Not in a corner
Just unbounded.
Time stopped racing.
The hamster stopped running.
Home and hearth
Invaded my heart.

This morning I awoke
knowing that there
Is nothing that can
contaminate
the magnificent
human spirit,
which has been
reignited by a
sacred spark.

The Book of Love and Life

In this book of love and life
some chapters we write,
some characters we meet
on days, the protagonist
on others, the antagonist
to plot, to plan, so tedious
as the plot was never
the bigger plan.

We gather our friends.
We label our enemies.
Lines are drawn, lines are blurred,
minds once made,
but minds have changed.

We draw from history.
We create a new story.
We pass it on to our progeny
We fall in love.
We fall out of love.
We falter in pain.
We rise again.

When we meet our needs,
we want more
desire burns
because others have more.
We compare:
the tallest, the highest
the greatest, the smallest, the fastest,
a never-ending test.

Like u-boats, we swirl
restless, unmoored
adrift.
Vast is the ocean
And left right there
in plain sight,
we have always known
what is right,
like a compass never lies
north or south
east or west,
like the moon is still the light
on a dark night,
even when she disappears
even when she is out of sight,
like the truth of a bud
is to find a way
to bloom, to flower
to then pave
the way for other flowers.

The Story of an Immigrant

I spoke to my parents yesterday
about my new identity,
a result of
forms and other factors,
of interviews and tests,
of learning the history
and the laws,
of states acquired
and identifying borders,
of knowing rights and wrongs,
of the past and present,
of what constitutes the constitution
the wisdom of founding fathers
and the enduring mothers.

We also spoke of the heart that
knows no boundaries,
where the colors of orange,
green, white, red, and blue dance,
of chakras, stars, and stripes,
turmeric, neem blend with sage and rosemary
in the fields of marigolds and wildflowers
where the elephant and the buffalo graze
and the hawk and peacock take their flight.

As I sat amongst rows of foreigners
each carrying stories from lands
near and far,
immigrants, immigrants, immigrants all,
of departures and arrivals
old ways and new life.
I listened to the children
who were invited to speak.
The young addressed the elders
in their clear, clean, earnest voices.
they told us what it meant to be born
in this country.
Right hand raised,
I took the sacred oath
to honor and defend,
to voice and participate,
to give and to receive,
to defend, to protect,
to preserve,
to serve.
For we are indivisible,
her and I,
you and I,
a merging of my two identities
the melting of so many souls.

The River of Stories

One day when you finally stop running,
You realize so many have been holding
And passing batons along the way.
You recall faces you hold dear
Some are far, and some are near,
Lives that intersect in different ways
Sometimes for a brief moment,
Sometimes for a little longer,
Some still present, others departed.

But what is presence other than
A collection of wisp-like memories,
A recalled fragrance,
An essential conversation
Brought back years later, like the retrieval
Of long-lost treasure
That could have happened
In the midst of the mundane,
One morning at the breakfast table
Or one evening when the moon was full,
When time-lagged and the urgent
Took a backseat to the important?

BE STILL MY HEART

This river of souls
That runs through us
In turns, placid, turbulent
Raging through time
No longer held back
By landlocked boundaries,
We are a collection of stories,
Where nothing is forgotten
Just kept hidden,
Of repeatable awareness,
Of voices new and old,
Past and present,
Trying to be heard
Trying to predict a worthy future.

Intentionality

i

I dust away the
irritations of yesterday,
and
greet this day
with its chirping birds
and fine green trees
with love in my heart.

ii

The task every day is to
love a little more,
judge a little less,
be more of myself
be less of someone else.

Shedding the excess weight
in the mind is the
hardest diet in the world.

iii

Take today and hug it tight.
Tell those you love how much they mean to you.
Then tell them why.
What is the point of holding LOVE back?
Let it flow so the waters nourish other souls.
This is the time of rebirth.
This is the way we resurrect.

iv

I looked up and saw the sky with a million lights
Who are you? What do you fear?
I looked down and felt the softness of the earth
What holds you? What do you lack?
The heart rushes in.
The head pushes back.
What did you forget? Where must you go?
One step aside. One step inside.
There it was.
There it is.
There it always will be.

V

The world from a window.
The window to the world.
Yesterday's grey skies
Make way to a blue, sun-kissed morning.

Wherever you are, whatever you are feeling,
May you never give up on yourself.
Anything rooted in fear will contract.
Everything planted with love will bloom.

The once bare limbed Redbud tree is sending
Out its magenta buds,
Which will then be followed by heart-shaped leaves.
What stayed in rest underground is getting ready to
send out shoots.
What calls out to you today?
Remove your inner resistance and give yourself
another chance.

The Best

The best is not yet to come.

It is not a place in the future,
Or a memory languishing in the past.

It is not a trade with the present,
Or always born in fair weather
Or a dream in fetters.

It is not waiting for planets to align,
Deferred for an auspicious time
When your ship can finally set sail.

It is anytime
Anyhow
Everyday
Any place
Anywhere
Everywhere
Always.

When the heart is curious
Skipping a beat
At the thought of something new,
Eyes in wonder
As another flower courageously blooms
Arching towards the sun,
With spirit wide open
Quite naive
Despite the wounds
Or the frequent bloodletting,
Surrendered with grace
Till your dying day.

The best is your constant.
Bet on yourself.

EPILOGUE

In the beginning, there was nothing. A blank slate.
The world was spring, and you and I, we had magic beans.
We were fed on promise and potential,
Gods who came down to earth and humans who
aspired to be like them,
The stories of heroes, of love ever after, of glass slippers
and indestructible capes,
young bodies and everlasting health.

Till life picks you up and time tears through.
That once perfect vision blurs and mistakes and
mishaps thread through the tapestry mingling
with celebrations and ceremonies.

Up and down.
High and low.
Inside out.
Outside in.
The sun rises and sets.
The colors of black and white bring in shades of grey.

Here is the arrival once again.
Where the heart that has been broken and mended
reaches out,
This time no longer afraid of rejection or expectation.

Be still, I say to my heart.
May we find the stillness in action.
For without stillness, we succumb to illness.
The mind is frantic, the heart is desolate, and the body
is without ease.

May we find peace within our courageous hearts.
May we find solace in our own sovereignty.
For when we are strong at the core, we can tame the
chaos at the edges.

Be still, I say to my heart.
Not still as in passive, lifeless, or senseless,
But be still in joy, in compassion, in love, in sweetness.
Be still in sorrow, grief, failure, anger, doubt, and
transition.
For through that stillness, lies forgiveness and mercy,
First for the self. Then for the other.
For here in this sacred space lies the invitation to
recognize grace.

Be Still My Heart

Acknowledgments

For me, poetry has always been a bashful bride. Each poem is a new adventure fraught with uncertainties.

The idea for a book would not have happened without the constant encouragement of so many friends and family.

To take it from an idea to a fully fleshed-out book could not have happened without the stellar steering of my publisher and editor, Andi Rosenau—a kindred soul whose mission is to help artists find their voice and platform on their own terms.

I am also tremendously grateful to Francine Marie-Sheppard, intuitive counselor and creatrix extraordinaire, for mentoring and directing the creative form for this book.

Finally, my heartfelt thanks to my brother, Arjun, and my sister, Meena, for providing feedback and Sarah Hannah Akbar for lending her eyes to the manuscript.

About the Author

Shaku Selvakumar discovered poetry fifteen years ago when a dear friend died unexpectedly. After that experience, it was easier for her to process and digest the unexpectedness of life through verse. When she is not writing poetry or dabbling in digital art, she loves practicing yoga, mentoring young adults, and exploring new hiking trails with her friends and family. *Be Still My Heart* is her first book of poetry.

Shaku is the founder of Activateen and has worked as a marketing and communications leader for various tech companies. She holds a Bachelor of Arts degree in literature, a post-graduate specialization in mass communications, and a Master of Business of Administration degree from the University of Bradford.

She lives in Austin, Texas, with her three daughters and "panda dog," a gorgeous Border Collie, Bernese Mountain, and Great Pyrenees mix.

You can find more information about Shaku at shakuselvakumar.com

Made in the USA
Coppell, TX
06 January 2022